At The Narrows

At The Narrows

POEMS

MEREDITH DAVIES HADAWAY

Word Poetry

Published by Word Poetry
P.O. Box 541106
Cincinnati, OH 45254-1106

ISBN: 9781625491237
LCCN: 2015931465

Poetry Editor: Kevin Walzer
Business Editor: Lori Jareo

Visit us on the web at www.wordpoetrybooks.com

COVER AND BOOK DESIGN by Diane Landskroener
COVER ART: detail from *A Dreamer* by Faith Wilson

Acknowledgments

The author gratefully acknowledges the following journals
and anthologies where the listed poems previously appeared,
sometimes in different versions:

The Book of Scented Things, "My Cat Knocks Over the Perfume"
Delaware Poetry Review, "Red Right Returning" and "Yellow
    Jackets"
Delmarva Review, "Blizzard" and "Heavenly Bed" and "On
    International Waters"
Fledgling Rag, "Blessing of the Animals," "Homeostasis," and
    "In the Middle of an Ice Storm, I Take my Cat Chloe to be
    Cremated,"
Folly, "Blade by Blade" "Hardware" and "Puddle"
Forge, "Pepper II" and "We Share 60 Percent of our DNA with a
    Banana"
Free State Review, "Ribbon"
Green Hills Literary Lantern, "Book of Omens"
Green Writers Press Magazine, "Even the Dark" and "Stink Bugs"
Hawaii Pacific Review, "To a Sycamore, Lately"
The MacGuffin, "Sight Unseen"
Mantis, "Sweeping Up the Bees"
McNeese Review, "The Lost Dolphin"
The Minetta Review, "End of the Line"
Nimrod International Journal, "Heron & Harp"
New Ohio Review, "At The Narrows"
Pearl, "Blank Pages"
poemmemoirstory, "Wash Day"
The Puritan, "Dear Amazon.com"
Qwerty, "In Season"
Rio Grande Review, "The Point"

Salamander, "A Cardinal, Hurling Himself at My Window"
Willow, "Monument"

I am grateful to the Maryland State Arts Council, the Rose
O'Neill Literary House at Washington College and the Virginia
Center for Creative Arts, for providing support during the
preparation of this manuscript.

Thanks also to readers and mentors, Jehanne Dubrow, Kim and
Frank Garcia, Jody Gladding, Marcia Landskroener, Kelly Lenox,
Carla Massoni, David McNaron, Erin Murphy, Amanda Newell,
Joan Smith, Barbara Buckman Strasko, and artistic collaborators,
Diane Landskroener and Faith Wilson.

Contents

III

For John

The Lost Dolphin

I found her once, as my boat drifted
in the late light of a small creek.

The wind had dropped, the way
it does when dusk settles. The last

grasses leaned over a mirrored edge.

Out of nowhere, she rose—breaking
the water's silver skin with her own, cresting

a puckered dorsal, then gone, beneath
circles of sky.

I wasn't certain I had seen her until she
arched again, swirling bubbles, puffing

a soft spume from her blowhole. I knew
she was off-course, so far from the bay

and the tide now threatening to strand us both.
But I stayed to watch her rise, submerge,

in slow orbit. Crickets chanting, a last
touch of sun. Her beautiful bulk

nudging wake through the marshgrass.
A lift, a dip—my hands pale as bone.

Here was the heart of the world,
shuttling its ancient breath between upper and

lower chambers. All muscle and shine, even
to the end.

I

How deeper than elsewhere the dusk is in your own yard.
Birds fly back and forth across the lawn
$\qquad\qquad\qquad$ *looking for home*
As night drifts up like a little boat.

—Charles Wright

Blank Pages

Everything begins as white—
the mug before the coffee fills it,

the sink before we pour the coffee out,
a lampshade, white before we turn

it gold with reading. *A mind of*
winter, Wallace Stevens wrote,

before we filled our minds with
Wallace Stevens.

A Cardinal, Hurling Himself at My Window

I'm told he sees his own reflection in the glass
as a competitor, a bird he must face down—

I'm not so sure. This morning, there's the sound
again—despite a sleep-soaked overcast,

the house still dark inside. *Thwap!*—a blast
of beak so loud it echoes all around

the kitchen where I dump my coffee grounds
into the sink—*tap, tap, tap*—a last

clump clings to the filter. *Thwap!*—another
protest. A fierce red warning at the blurred

edge between his world and mine. *Thwap!*—see?
My outline floats above the sill. His hovers.

The Book of Omens

"Falnama," Sackler Gallery

It's not the pictures I am
drawn to, but the words I cannot

read. The pattern-work,
calligraphy in foreign tongues

so that the swirl and swoosh of stroke
and ink are only that. Free

of the burden of message, letters
wheel across the page like

starlings, orbit
dots and dashes, turn

sideways on a chisel-edge
until they nearly

disappear—then
plummet, fat

and black, as if their density
alone portends an urgency.

Whatever it is has already come
to pass. Flies beyond

me, doubles
back, will come

again.

Facing   Pages

will be forever	severed. Likewise the
obverse, a chance	connection by back-
to-back circumstance.	Tossed, like tear-
off calendars,	page-a-day,
away, each stand-	alone, skimmed
screen by screen,	then gone
into the cyber-void	from whence
it came—like	"whence" itself,
a word that held	both time and
place until	it didn't any-
more. Will we need	mnemonics, as
we did before	we learned to
notch it all	in stone? Or will
our days be lighter	when we Kindle
them at both ends?	Or will they just

Spline

Not *anchor*—but the word we call a tiny
snip of something knotted in a string

to keep the end from slipping through
the soundboard of a harp. I lost not just

the thing but the word for it, while changing
a broken string. When I tried to pull the knot

in place the half-inch piece leapt into air.

An hour searching the rug turned up
nothing. Worse, I didn't know the name

of what was lost—a *stent*, a *spine*, a *splint*?
I only knew it seemed essential at the time.

Six months of vacuum cleaning and
scuffling shoes ensured the [   ] was gone.

Until the day we learned my husband
soon would lose his life.

He lay in a dark room. I went to the harp.

I knelt, hands sweeping twists and
turns in the rug's medallion, as if I'd find

some answer there where weavers once
had anchored warp and weft with knots.

Instead I found the little missing piece—
no worse for all the time it had been

lying there. Not quite as soft as *shrine*.
Something sharp like *split* or *splice*—

and when the word came back to me,
I hoped it was a sign.

Homeostasis

Each day I watch the pigeons flocking back
and forth across the bridge in a synchronistic

spin as if the sky were breathing in and
out each feathered body.

One white bird punctuates
the otherwise gray exhalation.

I remember reading that medieval kings
would keep a pure white bird to look

them in the eye when they fell ill, absorb
their sickness, then fly away, releasing all

disorder to the heavens. Driving home
at dusk I see the pigeon cloud repeat its

sweep across the sky—but this time,
no white bird.

I grip the wheel and feel the rise of dread
and hope in perfect equilibrium.

Another round of pigeon calisthenics.
Going out. Coming in. A simple exercise

to wing the heart through
each extremity.

White Dove in a Thrift Shop

Tucked between the racks of "buck-a-bag"
discarded clothes, I see a cage with a fat
bird perched so still I think it's stuffed.

That's Willie, says the shopkeeper.
*She turned out to be a girl, but we kept
the name.* The bird is sleek and solid white.

She perks up when her owner calls *C'mon,
Willie, don't be shy.* Willie stretches out
her pinioned wings and gives a useless flap.

She's spoilt, she says, *she's rotten.* Willie
gives a blink. *She shits in her water dish all
day long, when I'm here to clean it up.*

*But not one time when I'm not in the shop,
not once—we're closed on Sundays and
she knows it. Oh she's a special bird.*

I look for a price on a chipped teacup, turning
over the dinnerwear of the dead, I think.
I have no appetite to buy.

C'mon, Willie, show her how you laugh,
the owner says. *The White Doves aren't
supposed to laugh, but this one does.*

Willie starts to preen. And then a wild,
ethereal sound—more like a smothered
sob than laughter—startles me so

I almost drop the cup. *See there,*
I told you, she says. *She laughs*
real good.

Shopping Cart

I rarely see my neighbor, but every day the stolen
shopping cart that holds her treasure is parked

at the corner where her driveway meets my yard.
Arrangements nestle in the wire cage—a twist

of coat hangers, a changing sweep of glittery
scarves, a tinfoil castle, painted minarets

of bread dough and shellac—left there to absorb
the morning mist, the heavy sun of afternoon, still

visible in the moonlight's wild mix of shadows.
The little landscape changes with each new discovery

from the trash behind the junk store, a purple
vase, a shower cap to thwart the rain—and all

the other forces that devolve the scene. I pass
each day and think how much we are alike:

slow rust, precarious capture—ordering it all
around a heart-on-wheels.

Hat

The way it holds your head
  as if to keep your temple pulse
    in check, protect you from the
      desiccated glare of too much

out-of-doors, a guilty nod to
  where the real work happens—
    there beneath the brim of
      everything you cannot know,

a blinding edge. You have to
  hold it down to keep it from
    its natural urge to leap away
      from all attempts to make it

knowable. Faint odor of field
  and straw that never fades,
    no matter how tight the weave
      or dark the closet. Put it on and

feel the attic's heavy breath—
  the time that's packed behind
    you. A hat will fight the river
      wind unless you take it slow,

keep rhythm with the falling
  tide and stacked-up clouds of
    autumn. The air hangs hard
      around the house, the flowers

slump, the leaves are spotted brown or
missing altogether. Time to take the hat
back to the closet, where everything
will wait—as if we'll ever have the time.

Myotis Lucifigus

I want to apologize to the small
brown bats who orbited our nights

oblivious to backyard barbecues, long
walks by the river, the old man wheeling

his trash to the curb. They were willing
to let us proceed as if there were no bodies

hurling themselves from the attic when dusk
freed them from the hot stupor of their days.

Reeling like drunk birds they chased clouds
of gnats and slipped through our shadows.

*Bats are more closely related to people than
to mice*, I read. They have hair. They feed

milk to their young. Bats are not blind, despite
what lies we have told ourselves. They listen.

Each high-pitched cry comes back to say where
moths flutter, where wasps rest their wings.

Now the bats are leaving us. Palms open, like
sleepwalkers, we tiptoe through the blank spaces

where summer used to live. No cries, no echo—
only our small hearts chittering.

Yellow Jackets

We lunch outside beneath a fringed umbrella
to celebrate the autumn sun—still here.
Between the plates, I see a yellow jacket
creeping toward your can of soda.

Many years ago my boss told me about
a football game at a college in Ohio.
Beside him in the stands, a man was cheering
through the final down, gripping his beer.

Just as the score was turning, he took a swig
of froth that held a yellow jacket.
"Dead in ten minutes," my boss told me—
"he was allergic."

Thirty years have passed. My long-retired
boss has died a slower death. And something
in the light this time of year reminds
me how we cannot trust in warmth or even

sustenance. I watch you lift the Coke
and hold my breath. You take a sip
and swallow chill and effervescence.
Time out. A taste of the coming season.

Fruit Flies

They cloud around us everywhere
demanding what—a glass of wine?

Oh yes, they like the grape a bit
too much, and also apple cider.

The smell of fallen apples swells
the kitchen, where we've left

a small bowl on the counter. And
sure enough, they find their way,

drawn to the scent of earth's steamy
breath, a distant dream of green or

memory of the warm palm of a
picker. They gather on the rim

to peer into the cauldron of their
fate. Hundreds crowd the edge

to sniff the soup of everything
that's ever been an orchard—

its temptation, its sin. Eventually
they succumb to what's forbidden

and dive in. We all have limits.
Fruit flies can appear from nowhere,

swarm and spin, endure a climb, survive
a tumble—but they cannot swim.

Stink Bugs

Unwilling immigrants, all
overcoat and banded leg,
I find you pacing up and
down the edges of my
window pane.

Packed and shipped by
accident from some Asian port,
you gather here as if
a passing plane might
take you home.

One, overturned
on the ledge below, now
waves like an old uncle whose
body has become a burden too
heavy to set right.

Is it wrong to hate you?

Helpless, except your stink—
a pungent smell described as
like cilantro—meant to keep
the birds and lizards off
your back.

I cannot kill you, though I'm
told that liquid soap will do
the trick. Instead, I leave you
dreaming at the glass, where
an intermittent

buzz and flutter will remind
me how far away home is and
how we all want to go there and
how some people love

cilantro and others think
it tastes like soap.

Sweeping Up the Bees

wing over wing   a heap

      of brittle husks   tumbles

          ahead   of the broom's

rasp   each a tiny

      bloom of dust

that flutters   across

      my shadow   a riddle

        of wings   no industry   no

flight   no sting

      more potent

        than the whisper

of this   brush

Two Apples

Two apples in a bowl, cheek to
cheek, chin-on-chin, earthy

nuzzle of paradise and sin. Glow
with ripeness at dusk, smell

of orchard, tinge of rust. Stems
we twirled in search of love.

Sharp flesh and pithy core,
a cargo of seeds in rosy globes

that spread and flatten, pucker
and run, as two apples

become one.

Crow Funeral

Wind worries the feathers

      of those perched over

the fallen. All rise

      in one black breath

To a Sycamore, Lately

I cannot know the hundred
      springs when tiny leaves uncurled
            to grasp the sky, the summers

of humid bark and peeling days—
      I know nothing of your life, though
            I watched it end with ropes and saws

and men. I remember my first autumn
      at this river's edge, how I sat beside
            my father in a quilted shade you

made for us. He was old then, too,
      but no more so to me than you—both
            spreading limbs in the tinged air, there,

where you'd always been when
      the moon rose to touch the clouds, when
            the world turned silver, when

geese barked their lonesome cries across
      the flock, when they stopped.

II

In the middle of the road there was a stone.

—Carlos Drummond de Andrade
(trans. Elizabeth Bishop)

What I Did (Not) See

I did not see the green Jeep
parked in the oncoming lane.

It was a high bridge—where cars
do not stop—that I did not see.

There was a man, who walked
across the center line to reach

someone I could not see.

The cars slowed down to let
him cross. He was a handsome

man, the one I did not see, an
off-duty police officer, I later read.

He was concerned, I might
have guessed, if I could see

the open mouth that stumbled
over words I could not hear.

He was a handsome man who
drove a Jeep, his arms were tan,

his hair was very blond, I would
have noticed, had I seen him.

His tan arm stretched toward
the opposite rail where I did not

see a chain-link fence, nor
the woman straddling it.

I could have seen how awkwardly
she clung to either side, with one

leg hooked across the top and the other
dangling free, but I did not.

She had on jeans, I would have noticed,
and a green jacket and brown boots—

how one might dress to scale
a fence—I would have thought,

had I seen her. How she wrapped
her fingers through that mesh, so as

not to fall,

how the cars each kept their slow,
respectful, progress.

A lover's quarrel, I want to say,
he's here to talk her out of it.

How the wind troubled her hair.
I might have anchored it behind

her ears, since she had no hand
for the task.

Did I stop my car, put my thumb
on the knob to lower the far

window? I meant to ask did she
need my help — with the hair,

with the fence.

But at that moment, on the summit
of the bridge, she met me

eye-to-eye, and I went blind.

I did not see the rest—the water's
part and slide—the words

that spanned the billboards up ahead,
the iron sky behind.

At The Narrows

Now, when even midday sun holds shadows,
and only the wooden boats are left, bless
scarred hulls and splintered pilings.

Bless the hands that still twist eel into lines
of hard commerce. Bless the motor's stutter
declaring, *yes, we will go out.* Bless the foul

mud that peppers the gunnel, the ascent
of the bait, its twitch as it goes over the roller.
Bless the slow crab, too greedy for stink to see

the net coming and the basket, slats leaking
a scrabble of claws. *Wanda J, Alice Rose,
Edna*—grubby river angels, decks swollen

with rain, smelling of brine and rot, all divot
and slop—bless your deadrise, your hard
chine, your rudder. In the morning, all will

blur into mist. Crabs will begin their exodus
to deeper waters. We tell ourselves they will
be back. May this, too, be true.

Puddle

Thank you, puddle, for what you
did not become.

Instead, a still life, a snapshot of sky
that did not fall.

A blink of the eye in
the face of a storm.

A toe-dip, a leg-up, another
shot, a prayer,

a wrinkle, a nickel, a whiff
of singed hair,

Small sip of not-disaster, a taste
of metal and earthworms

but not
what comes after.

Even the Dark

And as we forgot the dark, we forgot even the rain.
                                    —Agha Shahid Ali

Forget the stars, forget the moon—even the dark is leaving us.
Instead of night, a halide afternoon. The dark is leaving us.

Peppered moth, your wings turned black to match the sooted bark,
turn back to your cocoon—everything dark is leaving us.

Windows, with your open throat, the breath of night's relief,
you may as well just shut the room. The dark is leaving us.

Extinguish candles, we don't need their little orbs. We kindle
clouds to shine all night. And so the dark is leaving us.

Only the blind now see what once made blindness tragic,
the long mystery, its black magic. Yes, even the dark—

Rain can't fall at night—instead it weaves through phony-day
to drop on one last place that wanted to be bright. All right.

Let there be light. Let us flutter in the glittering ash of spark
and blaze. Let us have our ways. We don't believe in the dark.

In Season

Rain-soaked morning, soft
      as my pillow, a dream of
            feather and gunshot.

Old Days

In the old days, we stuck candles in wine bottles—
Mateus or Chianti—and let the wax drip

down the neck and sides while we lingered over
meals of noodle casseroles made with cream

of mushroom soup. We smoked cigarettes in the
old days, sometimes menthols—Kools or

Salems—inhaling the tiny chill like a premonition.
In the old days, we drank instant coffee, laced

with chemicals to make it *instantly*, so we could linger
even longer and smoke more menthol cigarettes.

Nights were long in the old days; we drank more
coffee, opened another bottle of Chianti, watched

more wax join the blob that clung around the base
of the candle, which we poked with blackened

match heads from a Pep Boys matchbook. We
performed tricks in the old days, lighting matches

without removing them from the book, solving
riddles about snow shovels in only two moves.

Or sometimes we just lit matches—one by one—
to watch them flare before we dropped them on

our empty plates. In the old days we would talk.
There was always so much to say, in the haze of

candle wax and sulphur, sipping Nescafé. Every
word, still in its wrapper of possibility, held so much

time—and often we gave our sentences extra syllables
to stretch them further—strings of "uhs," "you knows,"

and "likes"—and this did not annoy us in the old days
because we still had hours and hours before we'd

hear the clink and rattle of the milkman, and in a final
puff of menthol, we would blow the candle out.

Hardware

Hammer, with its wounded
handle and [ironic] head

always at the ready for propping
up the weary edge of things

determined to fall down,
the clapboard siding, gapped

by heat and flood, the nails
refusing to settle

like [small] worries
of the sleepless mind, [keep] popping

up, protruding into dreams,
while the wind dizzies

the sycamores, scrapes
at shingles, and bangs

on the one [unbolted?] door.

Robbery

They come at dawn, through an unlocked door.
Steal the morning sun's expanding rays
before they steal my love of darkness, raised
windows, night air, whispering furnace. Before
they take the shadowed walls, patterned floors
the skylight's strange illusions, rain's crazed
murmuring. *What's missing?* the unfazed
cop has asked. (The answer he ignores.)

They leave me here alone with locks and keys.
A light that springs with every passing skunk
illuminates one slice of night, a bluff
of waving limbs in silhouette, a tease
to warn me back inside a house that's shrunk
and shrinking. *Everything*, soon enough.

Blizzard

Whiteout, they call this, because blowing
snow eclipses any view except

the ice mosaic at the window.

Between gusts, I see flecks of sky
and river driven sideways, two gulls

muscling something they think
is edible from the water's frozen lip.

Inside, everything is also white. The walls rise
like drifts beside me as my feet

sink further into the pile of the carpet.

House gone dumb, without the
hum of electric current.

*Blizzard conditions can occur with just one
inch of snow*, the forecaster said. *It's*

about wind and visibility. The opposite
of a hard winter—a soft winter.

One that billows its blankness around
you, with hospital corners

to tuck you in.

Incandescent

The first day on earth without
you, the sun rose strangely bright—

lumens, you told me, is how we
measure light. You were turning

a bulb in its socket, swapping out
the darkened head with a twisted

tube of cooler white. *Just not the
same*, you said, as the glass

shattered in the trash can. So much
heat from such a slender

filament. But one by one as each
burns out, we'll have to find

our way through colder afternoons
and dimmer nights.

February, Middle of the Night

after John M. Ridland

No, this is aging: A sly moon
on the run from the sycamore's
clutch of branches spills over
the window sill, shattering

into slivers of silver. A heap
of cast-off pillows collapsed
by the side of the bed.

Star light, star bright—not
now, disheveled wanderer—I'm
too tired. Disarray my
sleep, scatter redundant

covers, but then let daylight
straggle back like a reluctant
child, begging for one more

story before bedtime.

Stendhal Syndrome

"a psychosomatic illness causing rapid heartbeat, dizziness, fainting, confusion, and even hallucinations when a person is exposed to art"

The layering of cobalt and zinc,
over gesso, turpentine, linen stretched

across wood, hanging on
gypsum and brick, the influx

of nitrogen, with its soul
mate, oxygen,

daylight wavering, photons
striking pooling

lipids, an onslaught of peptides
aligned for ex-

change, a signal that beckons
and beckons, then begs

you to shift—from one foot
to the other—

your weight

as cadmium, viridian,
cerulean swirl,

and sienna burns.

La Bella Principessa

After the portrait now believed to be by Leonardo da Vinci

Experts ponder hatching, *pentimenti*, where
chalky layers of pigment hide the fingerprint

of its maker. For so many years there were
only questions. Now we hear there are clues.

Bianca Sforza, we learn that you were not
a princess but a child who stared pale-eyed into

a future you would not live to see. A girl
betrothed—the way that daughters were—

as tribute to a man you'd never met.
The artist was left-handed, we can tell.

But who unwound the ribbons from your long
blond hair? Who cupped the breast that barely

swelled before an unborn child killed you?
Scholars spend their days debating knotwork,

interlacing patterns in the costume and the caul.
The ragged edge of vellum tells them that Bianca

was a portrait someone razored from a book.
So small, the little face revealed when the exhibit

comes to Gothenberg. They film the man in gloves
who lifts her from a black valise and places her

inside a case. With an exaggerated twist, he turns
the lock as if to say now she is *safe*.

"And There was Light" the show is called.
Bianca stares in profile through the haze of colored

chalk. A fingerprint rubbed into vellum.
A palm print on her neck.

In the Middle of an Ice Storm, I Take My Cat Chloe to be Cremated

Wrapped in plastic, in a taped-up
cardboard box, she

gives a final twitch
from the heat that's still

escaping.

My heart curls up
by the fire.

Heavenly Bed

This is the afterlife. A towering
kingdom of feather and

down. Endless pillows.
Where nothing is required of you

except surrender to the plump
comforter. Hear the sweet singing

of the sheets, tone-on-tone around
each mitered corner. The Jacquard stripe

that holds you, hems you, pampers
you, until the sateen finish.

Why wait to die, before you wake?
Turn out the light and join me

here in the final thread count.

"We Share 60 Percent of our DNA with a Banana"

Origins of Man exhibit, Museum of Natural History

This explains so much. Why
King Kong fell for blond
Fay Wray; why everything

has strings attached; why we're
drawn to rum but cringe at the
sound of blenders; why we say

someone untested is still *green*;
why we feel safer in a bunch;
why we think banana peels

are funny; why Basho chose
to name himself *Banana*
for the kindred plant that grew

beside his hut—why when we
lose control, we go bananas.

My friend tells me bananas
saved her life. A childhood
illness back in Africa, a tortured

stomach and wailing
mouth that nothing could
put right until—

O brave banana brother! Unlike
your fallen apple cousin, you
do not tempt but sacrifice.

No wonder banana clusters spring
from *hearts* and grow in tiers
called *hands*. Like you,

our skins are tough, our
souls are tender. And yes, like
you, we bruise so easily.

Without

        you, the house becomes a leaky
tub, a river of rust, a crooked
                door—come off its
hinges—windows painted
        shut above the listing
                countertops, charred burners—

        But listen, the wooden floor still creaks
when I walk across its
        web of scars, a patched-up
                hole where a cookstove
used to sit, beside a chimney
        crumbling back
        to ash.

Blade by Blade

Vermont

The night the wind from the lake blew
strange music through the rented cottage,

a bleating scale, like a French
horn player testing his lip

[a drug-crazed kid inflicting his broken
days] our broken nights

[the separate explanations of our sleep-
tossed minds]

a plaintiff repeating his claim as if repetition
alone could win us over.

All night the air swept through
the rafters [banging the shades against

the sills] puzzling our dreams in ways we'd try
to describe over breakfast,

while outside and just beyond our
view, a rusty windmill leaned on its

rickety scaffold.

End of the Line

The apparition of these faces in the crowd;
petals on a wet, black bough.

The dead still ride the subway. They orbit—like the guy in the
song who is stuck beneath Boston—on the Apparition
Express. *Don't say I never take you anywhere,* the late husband of
Mrs. Died-Last-Week tells his reunited bride. Yes, these
are the lost we long for. Children press their faces
to the tinted glass of the windows. Others fidget in
the hard, black seats. Everyone waiting for the
stop that never comes. It's a restive crowd—

You mean restless, says my eighth grade English teacher, petals
drooping from her primrose hat. She's moved on—
I should have guessed. What I wouldn't give for a
chance to breathe again her talcum and press the wet,
rouged cheek. But already she's buttoned her long black
coat and left me behind to puzzle—*branch, limb, or bough?*

Dear Amazon.com Customer

As someone who has purchased
books by William Shakespeare, you
might like to know that
Hamlet: Safe for the Whole Family
to Read Aloud will soon be
released in paperback.

In this version, nobody dreams and
nobody dies. No scheming uncles, poison
swords, no duels, no loss,
no suicide.

Customers who bought safe titles by
William Shakespeare might also want:

D.H. Lawrence, *Lady Chatterly's Best Friend Forever*;
Joseph Conrad, *Heart of Night-Night*;
and Unknown Author, *Who's Afraid of Beowolf?*

The Point

It is Seurat that stops me drifting through the crowd
     of museum-goers on a Free Night at the MoMA.
Those landscapes filled by tiny pricks of light that open up
        the sky and vibrate, illuminating time and space outside
the frame, the length and breadth and height of walls
     now going on forever in expanding molecules that flood my
       mind and carry it—awash in radiance—down
          the fifth-floor escalator.

Outside, struggling through the slickened streets
     with an umbrella shield (not from the rain but from
the bobbing spokes of hundreds of umbrellas) as we trudge
        toward some address I do not recognize, fording streams
that puddle ankle-deep at every crossing until we find ourselves
     in night sky bright as daylight, pixilated, wired, electric dance
       of photons so surprising that I stop here—

concrete shining wet beneath my feet—and tell myself
     I finally get it: this is Times Square. This is Times Square.

Bloom

The river swirls
    where a large carp
        wheels into shadow.

III

And again: summer will last
No more than an hour
But let our hour be
Vast as the river.

—Yves Bonnefoy
(trans. Hoyt Rogers)

Red Right Returning

This time of year the sun goes
down, downriver, one last ember

glowing sideways to my left.
Other times it settles somewhere else.

It slips away all fall, then climbs
back slowly in the spring.

What's that sailors say about red
skies at night?

How easy to believe in words—
how much harder to believe in gas and rocks.

This is the miracle: that the sun wanders
by me every day and when it

sinks—somewhere on my left tonight—
you can be pretty sure it will

re-surface on my right, whether
I rise early to watch it light the angles

of the sky or stay in bed to feel it
blaze my bones.

Too

*Stressed form of to prep., which in the 16th cent.
began to be spelt too. [OED]*

Five hundred years ago, a preposition paused
and told a second o, *oh yes.*

Too, it's back in fashion to begin
your sentence with this largesse.

What a comforting word—
so little, such excess.

River Otters

Though I've never seen them, please
    let them be here.
        Small gods of

happiness that somersault
    through the river's upper
        reach. I want to hear them

chuckle and romp. I want
    to see them float backward,
        fish flopped across bellies,

fur ruffed at their throats.
    Let there be breakfast for
        otters and naps in the sun.

Let them wheel in the
    current, pumping webbed
        toes. Let them slap at the

tide as they tumble. Let them
    hide when I churn my boat
        upriver. Enough to imagine

them—holding their breath
    beneath the large, sad surface—
        when my shadow passes.

Ribbon

Ribbon serves no purpose,
except to designate a gift.

Looped around its serpent
self in ritual temptation

Ribbon says: *You won't possess this
treasure, until I let it go.*

My favorite ribbon shimmers
like a negligee. Its peek-a-boo

translucence invites (denies) desire,
possibility: now you see it, now you—

pull one end and ribbon drops its
prohibition and becomes all

exhibition, like the satin strap that
slides from collarbone to elbow.

Ribbon holds our bare demise
within its crisscross, twisted tie:

everything you think you want,
already have, will never have.

Inside its silken arms is [   ] only
a diversion from the disarray

of each disheveled minute, every
hour's sloppy kiss, the scent of wet

pavement, the one true gift.

Pepper II

No one knows why
Pharaoh Ramses II was
found with peppercorns
stuffed up his nose, but

we have our suspicions.

After 30 years of reign
he made himself a god,
and, yes, his corpse
survives—was flown to

Paris under an Egyptian
passport noting
*Occupation: King
(deceased)*—not God
and sadly, not immortal.

Unless you are a god,
don't shove pepper up
your nose—when you
sneeze, air leaves your

nose at 100 miles per
hour. Try not to
squander it.

Birthday

Despite wars and global warming,
no sunscreen, fast runs over shallow
water, ignoring all the warnings,

to be turning sixty means the end
of *someday*, stepping stones, a résumé,
the end of middle age—the end of

middle—the end of waist and waste,
the end of whining. Now wine tastes
of blackberry and smoke; friends

from years ago feel impossibly close;
words we never said return in deep
voices of the beloved dead.

As the river grows small, I see its
cratered edge, a scarf of stars
billowing overhead.

Elegy with Airport & Elephant
For RAM

I see your ashes rising off the runway,
sucked into a turbine, flown above
a patchwork mania of one-way
streets, mismatched meds, and love—

more medication—*all madness*, you
would say—now miniature, in patterns, math,
a tidy music that your mind can tune to
as you streak across the flight path.

Back on earth, we wonder, look for clues.
I scroll your online posts and find—still living—
a photo of a baby elephant at a local zoo.
For Meredith, your only comment outliving

you. You could not know I'd see it days
beyond our spinning on a mutual planet. Years
ago I said I'd always wanted one. And hey—
it's here. A barely-wrinkled brow and folded ears

a patch of startled hair, a twitch of tail.
An immature and trusting heart, not yet
cursed with infallible memory, mammoth scale.
How like you never to forget.

Wash Day

The dead are decomposing everywhere—
you can smell their slurry of rain and paperwork,
cold tea, apricots weeping in damp air.
Their odors cling to vacant sweaters, lurk
in cars, swivel in office chairs. Remind
us we must eat, wrestle, mate—collect
the laundry. As I stuff the sheets you left behind
into the washer, they bloom again the wrecked
perfume of you.
                    Despite detergent
and a splash of bleach, nothing comes clean—
it all tumbles from the dryer in waves of urgent
heat. Fold—crease—repeat. Between
each stretch of white, the small scents float—
leather, orange, ash, and Ivory soap.

By Any Measure

My brain, no help,
confuses household
objects—the dangling
measuring spoons
I snatch up thinking
they're my keys—

finds all this semblance
in unrelated stuff.
I leave the bolted
door and pour a tiny
mound of salt into
the quarter-teaspoon.

Just enough.

Monument

The body cannot be fooled—
will carry its burden only

so long before giving
it back. Limbs become

the twisted trunks of the
cedar tree by the graveyard

gate. Hair splinters
into silver bark.

The heart at last has legs
to stroll about the edge

of what is visible.
The tongue, grown wings,

takes flight but doesn't
stray. Instead it lingers

in the throat of a small
bird who calls from the top

of a stone monument.

Perched on the outstretched
hand of a concrete angel,

the body's song is feathery
and light. The angel on her

obelisk points up.
But her shadow slants

across the stone, always
journeying downward,

inching its way home.

Blessing of the Animals

Dogs and cats, three white mice and a
ferret wait for Father Tom to sweep
across the lawn in Holy Robes.

He stops to pat a furry head and scratch
a chin. Here and there he throws a bone
of praise to the owner for clever tricks

or perfect manners. Mostly it's children who
strangle-hold a web of leashes but there's
the octogenarian with her silver cat, the visiting

New Yorker's Cairn, and the mud-splattered
horse-mucker holding back her
Jack Russell terrier.

One by one by each, a blessing.
Father Tom has seen it work. No need
to look for evidence of soul in this milk-bone

menagerie. What could be more human
than their halitosis, shedding coats and
endless hankering?

Clouds shift behind the steeple and a moist
breeze threatens but Father Tom, unruffled,
kneels beside a white-faced Golden

who is too crippled to rise. She gives
the priest a patient look and licks
the proffered hand as if to say:

Go with dogs, my friend. Learn to leave
behind the things you can't retrieve.

My Cat Knocks Over the Perfume

Osmanthe Yunnan, Hermes

And now my desk, alive with *apricot-jasmine-tea*,
refuses dreary tasks—the cat has dressed it up
in sticky notes and shiny tacks, paper clips dangling
from an open drawer, a smear
of Wite-Out winking. This cat's all *freesia*
and freedom. She's not just thinking *sachet*,
but away, away—*sashay*, as she glides
down the stairs—no work today. She's *translucent*,
She's *clear* and, furthermore, she's out of here.
                              Gone now,
till after dusk, strutting the streets in search
of leather and musk. *That's it*, I say in the morning.
She only rubs a scented paw behind her
ear and yawns so wide I see her missing tooth.
So much for beauty. So much for truth.

Sight Unseen

I went blind yesterday during

lunch—a migraine, triggered

by whatever it is that triggers

migraines. Strange ocular

shimmerings block the center

of your vision, so you can only

see part of the person you are

having lunch with—one eye

and half a mouth. And this is

odd and distracting, especially

since the restaurant is full of

people going on with their meals,

normal and whole, while I'm

watching half-a-mouth gobble

rare tuna from half-a-fork, a

tiny tongue of arugula sliding

across half-a-lip before

disappearing.

A certain name comes up in

conversation and half-a-nose

wrinkles to indicate at least a

bit of something like disdain.

When I mention that I'm only

seeing half of everything around

me, one eyebrow arches in

concern, though I'm almost

certain that the other brow

remained aloof. So I ate my

half-a-lunch, ignoring

everything that was lost in

shade and shimmer, tossed

       my credit card on the table

(we split the check), stuck

       one arm inside one sleeve

and waited for the other arm

       to come along, the way

I knew it would.

On International Waters
for Chris

Precarious as chardonnay in glasses balanced
on the gunwale—though there was no wake
to tip them, not another boat in sight.

A blonde head bowed to weigh each word
against another, trading trust for trust
because, she said, we were *on international waters.*

Meaning we could safely talk right through
the tide that nudged our drifting boat upriver—
a mile or more before we saw how far we'd come.

Golden—like the final blaze before the sun
disperses marsh grass into ember—
her hair, the wine, the confidence that time

would heal all hearts and end all conflict.
Still sipping wine, we laughed and toasted
to find the river had returned us to the

very dock we left—*a miracle*, we said,
it must have been the lack of
wind or maybe river angels.

If we knew then what force could
stop that courteous flow—or pluck
us from the water altogether—

we'd have done the same: the fading
chime of glass on glass in the starlit
sparkle—to seal a pact—all those secrets,

the only thing we get to keep.

Heron & Harp

I drag my harp across the gapped
terrain of pier—a hundred feet with nothing
underfoot but slats of air and swirling tide—

and place the harp in front of me to play
"The Water Is Wide," a sort of joke here,
where the channel is so narrow.

A few notes into the song: a squawk.
Flying low, a heron glides across
the river's edge to land beside me.

Head tucked so he can stare me down
from his perch on a piling—

summoned by the strange cascade of frequencies—
or did he mistake the arching frame for another
large and gawky bird?

I keep the tune going, a slow air
we would call it, as the oscillations rise,
and then retreat, leaving

song and bird, the harp and me suspended
in a pulse, a wave, a measure
where the water is wide enough
to hold us all.

About the Author

An award-winning poet and teacher of ecopoetry, Meredith Davies Hadaway is the author of two previous collections, *Fishing Secrets of the Dead* (2005) and *The River is a Reason* (2011), from WordTech Communications. She is the poetry editor for *The Summerset Review*. Hadaway has received fellowships from the Virginia Center for Creative Arts, an Individual Artist Award from the Maryland State Arts Council, and multiple Pushcart nominations. She holds an MFA in Poetry from Vermont College of Fine Arts. Hadaway served as the 2013-14 Rose O'Neill Writer-in-Residence at Washington College. She lives on the Chester River, on Maryland's Eastern Shore.

CPSIA information can be obtained
at www.ICGtesting.com
Printed in the USA
FFOW02n2036290415
13065FF